the elephants are asking

poems by
Karen Neuberg

Glass Lyre Press

Copyright © 2018 Karen Neuberg
Paperback ISBN: 978-1-941783-43-6

All rights reserved: except for the purpose of quoting brief passages for review, no part of this book may be reproduced or transmitted in any form or by any means, electronic or mechanical, including photocopying, recording, or by any information storage and retrieval system, without permission in writing from the publisher.

Cover art: © Sasin Tipchai
Author photo: Leslie Prosterman
Design & layout: Steven Asmussen
Copyediting: Linda E. Kim

Glass Lyre Press, LLC
P.O. Box 2693
Glenview, IL 60025
www.GlassLyrePress.com

For my grandsons, Gabe and Seth,

and for all the children

Acknowledgments

The author gratefully acknowledges the editors of the publications in which the following poems first appeared, sometimes in earlier versions and/or with different titles:

Bluestem Magazine, "Little Wakes"
Canary, "Old Game"
eco-poetry.org, "Climate Lag Time" and "the elephants are asking"
Forge, "With Bird's-eye View"
Free Verse: A Journal of Contemporary Poetry & Poetics, "Möbius"
Gyroscope, "In a Numbness"
The Maynard, "What Seems Solid"
Muddy River Review, "Quality"
Möbius, the Poetry Magazine, "Occupy Today"
The New Verse News, "If all I have is a teaspoon"
Poetry 24, "Bystander," "Perpetuity"
Poets for Living Waters, "Evidence"
S/tick, " … "
Whirlwind, "Information"

With great pleasure, I thank Cynthia Atkins, Patricia Carragon, Bob Heman, Cindy Hochman, Lissa Kiernan, Jesse Lunin-Pack, Alan Neuberg, Liz Neuberg, Leslie Prosterman, Alison Stone, and Alexandra van de Kamp, who encourage and inspire me. And Gabe and Seth, who remind me of what's important.

To my Monday lunch group, friends for many decades—Mary Ann, Susan, Naomi, Rosie, Rifka, Ange: thanks for the many hours listening to me go on about poetry, art, the creative process, and the environment; and sharing your thoughts, concerns, ideas, and enthusiasm.

And special thanks to Ami Kaye and the Glass Lyre Press staff for their belief in this manuscript and their expertise and support that made publication possible.

Contents

Acknowledgments — v

I

Möbius — 3
In a Numbness — 4
Evidence — 5
Bystander — 6
Climate Lag Time — 7
On Being Here Now — 8
Perpetuity — 9
Quality — 10
Information — 11
the elephants are asking— — 12

II

Old Game — 17
Call to — 18
What Seems Solid — 19
Occupy Today — 20
If all I have is a teaspoon — 21
Little Wakes — 22
With Bird's-eye View — 23
… — 24

Notes/Bibliography — 25
About the Author — 27

I

...for we are part
Of every rock and bird and beast and hill,
One with the things that prey on us, and one with what we kill...
—Oscar Wilde, Excerpt from
"Panthea: We Are Made One
with What We Touch and See"

Möbius

Where the wild concerns ache into language—almost—then dissolve. You know it's there. Knocking. Scratching. Nudging with its cold nose for attention. More than attention—longs to rise, shake loose confinement's dust, be visible. It swears that's where it can be fixed. Among the recognized. Cup in hand. Tired eyes. A whole world on its back. Back bleeding. You want to help; you do. But pulling it up—you just know—will tear your heart apart. You've only got one heart. Small beating thing. Cold nose ...

In a Numbness

Are these hours
crazy, or are we?
Looking the other way—
away from too much
disturbance and toward
what is still
splendid or diverting.
Between this breath
and those not yet
taken, when effects
will be felt. When
is too late
and what to do
before. I notice
what I notice.
It's everywhere.
Even when I think
I'm not looking.

Evidence

Start today as always. Time is matter.
Pluck, stitch. Threads of moment

a darling addiction. Collects in the wisdom
of the oceans.

Evidence is crude
& wide. Watch & watch more.

No time for complacency. Weeping
is not sufficient.

Let's learn something here. Now.
Dammit! Let's at least look.

Bystander

i.
At the very least:
junk floating

in our oceans.

ii.
While it is still possible
to choose to not look

it is impossible to continue
to not see.

Climate Lag Time

Reports arriving from air, land, sea

    Another oil spill/pipeline rupture
    Coral reefs dying around the world
    Red algae in the arctic snows
    Bees and other flying insect populations declining worldwide
    Nuclear and methane leaks
    Hottest days on record
    Forest wildfires globally, ash & smoke choking cities
    Microplastics in the deep, open oceans
    Once-in-a-thousand-year rains
    Sinking land, rising seas
    Thousands killed, millions displaced by storm-caused floods around the globe
    Fire tornadoes …

overturning tranquility.

On Being Here Now

In little towns across. In cities
where glass rises into sky, confuses birds.
Where workers pour out of confined spaces,
meet in the doorways of cubicles.
In a heartstring. Navigation in changing
climates. Diversion after diversion.
Extinction debt lag time.

Perpetuity

Unrelentingly,
water pours
for the next 100 years,

swollen with radiation.
The fish have not been told.
Nor the birds warned.

Clouds lift mist & vapor,
rain it back down
10,000 & more miles away.

The children are swaying
in our arms. They cannot drink
the milk. Mothers help them

put on their masks. Fathers
weep. Whoever remains
will hear the stories,

which will grow like cancers.
Whatever remains
will glow in the dark

bone by bone.

Quality

Just for starters
as you take your next breath
and then exhale:

diesel, formaldehyde,
benzene, particulate matter, ground-
level ozone …

Earth is round and currents travel
around. What blows will reach
everywhere.

And we haven't even talked about
what's happening to our waters.

Information

> *Everyone gets so much information all day long that they lose their common sense.*
>
> —Gertrude Stein

I see another spectacle blocking my view,
another fad slipping into my bed.
The cave walls are filled with conflicting shadows
demanding attention in urgent & dazzling tones.
How small respect has become. It fits our eyes like drones,
while entertainment pumps up our need to be amused.
I feel strings attaching to my heart, tugging me away from what I used to know.
I'm diverted by a spin of words that cover over and are covered by.
Pack of lies. Pack of truths. Information pours
and pours, burying us beneath ourselves.

the elephants are asking—

and the bees and the bats, the prairie dogs, the lemurs, the dolphins—one in six species—
asking!

And the coral reefs, the rivers & oceans, the islands & shorelines—asking!

And the aspen, the redwood, sequoia, the boreal, the rainforests—asking!

And the baby toes wiggling free in spring and summer, and the baby-plump arms, fat cheeks, trusting eyes—
asking!   Asking!

Even God is asking.

II

Kill me / when the names / for animals and sky / replace the animals and sky
—Alison Stone, "The Emperor"

Old Game

In yet-to-be hours, the remaining
children play the old game.

Milling around each other,
they jump and lumber, walk on all fours,

leap, roll, sniff, hug, flap arms,
and make assorted noises—

snorts, barks, buzzes, grunts, trumpets,
roars, low- and high-pitched cries—

until, one by one, they clutch
themselves and fall.

When all are down, another child
sprinkles them with powder

said to contain ground
horn and tusk, beak and claw,

while reciting in a solemn voice
names memorized by heart:

Whale, bat, bee, tiger, falcon, bobcat,
wildcat, zebra, gray wolf, jaguar, dolphin, giraffe,

manatee, terrapin, ocelot, elephant, gorilla, polar bear,
rhinoceros, hippopotamus, orangutan.

And with each name said,
a child raises an arm.

And this is the old game the children play.
And its name is *Sorrow*.

Call to

There are dangers I—*we*—tread
as though we're in a slow-rising flood.

I say this without irony that real flash-
flooding is occurring in an abundance

of once-in-a-thousand-year rainfalls,
the speed of them leaving us

unprepared to flee beforehand.
This is not an understory

to anything; it is
what it seems. Recurrent

changes challenging our ways & means
to get beyond just coping.

I tell you this not because I want to
disrupt your sense of well-being.

I suspect, like mine, it already is.

What Seems Solid

We're holding what seems solid
enough, although we're aware
close by might be crumbling,
and we quickly think *cookies*,
which leads to a lively conversation
about particles, and we think *strings*
and we think *theory*, and we're relishing
our clever minds and congratulating
ourselves, no longer thinking
winners but glad to be among the *placers*;

and then, gradually, we become aware
of the rumbling sound coming out
of everywhere and there's no time to think,
it's time to act, and whatever is coming
has already risen past our knees,
but we don't think *apocalypse*,
for we never believed that story,
but somehow the word is roaring in our ears.
And we think again *time to act*. Yet we're standing
here thinking and saying it, and we're not acting.

Occupy Today

My hiccup sobs are drawn across
this rough-hewn world. Look at me,
my sparkle waterlogged with disproportion.
Forgive me. Forgive
my persistent worry, my lack
of courage, my haggard eyes.
I have seen falling
continue to increase its pace.

I've also seen the newborn just washed
and combed, and I still believe in the redux
miracle called *hope*. I just can't find it,
and I'm sinking in the search.
Some days I want only
my mother. Some days I want to wrap
my arms around the world. I see
the future falling at accelerating speed.

Let me not drown in the dry heaves of resignation.

If all I have is a teaspoon

with a nod to Amos Oz

and if there's a calamity; say, a raging fire,
then I'll carry my teaspoon
filled with water and I'll pour it on
the raging fire and I'll go back and get
more water and that's what I'll do,
unless I find a bucket to fill and pour,
or a power hose to flush it all away,
and I will never stop helping
the greening to return.

Little Wakes

Dreams she's in someone else's dream
where a waterfall is spilling fast
while unsuspecting boaters row placid waters
above, paddling the distance from shore,
enjoying their place in the moment,
happy to be under the sun & upon the sun-flecked
expanse in their various boats, alone
or courting, or with spouses & children
whom they admonish playfully not to lean
too far over the side, and agree, yes,
the water is cool …

and everyone is looking
at the wrong strand, the one back there,
or mesmerized by reflections on the surface,
while they row toward that which roars,
still unaware of the dream they will tumble
into, not their own but the one someone else
has already lost control of.

With Bird's-eye View

I can tell you I've fallen onto the critical
stage after the stage itself has fallen
into the overlap of real & imaginary.
De-centered in the movement
of information, I want to hold reality
still enough to be held without invention, without the sea
of stimulation fusing aftermath & explanation.
I'm standing in a standstill, opening a book, studying its map
trying to glean events with bird's-eye view,
wanting to understand what I can do, then do it.

. . .

It's never quite found, that's all—and that's a lot. Though it feels almost discernible, there, under a pile of years that includes all the old socks missing in the wash. And more, of course—like the times I didn't lift the baby when she cried. She's a grown woman now; her babies no longer babies. I long to tell her. But tell her what?

And what of that collection rising to the ceiling about to hit the fan? Does it include the world? The newest and the oldest wars of my particular, or of any, lifetime? Can this become a cave in which to contemplate, meditate, reflect, resolve? The what? The how to find, to speak with clarity, to say as authentically

as moon casting light upon us. It doesn't take her illumination to know some rivers are too slick and filled with swill to sustain life. The animals we've held dominion over now extinct, or nearly so. The air we breathe, the food we eat—killing us. But then, isn't that where we're headed anyway? Or is it just me. Here, near an ending of one kind at least, or of the total, I don't know.

But I do seek to know how all that's passed through me fits in ways I struggle to convey. A richness and a poverty side by side. A rapture and a keening twisted like a rose and briar. The joyful song in some children's laughter. The tears of others falling ceaselessly. The thing as humans we must do, or not.

Notes/Bibliography

from "**Quality**":

United States Environmental Protection Agency. "The EPA lists the toxins in the air." www.epa.gov/ttn/atw/188polls.html

from "**Climate Lag Time**":

abcNews. "Oil Spill News," listed in reverse chronological order, abcnews.go.com/topics/news/oil-spill.htm?page=2

Bearak, Max. *The Washington Post,* "Attention is on Harvey. But flooding has killed thousands this month in other countries, too." August 29, 2017, https://www.washingtonpost.com/news/worldviews/wp/2017/08/29/attention-is-on-harvey-but-flooding-has-killed-thousands-this-month-in-other-countries-too/

The Economist, "Methane leaks a dirty little secret." July 23, 2016, www.economist.com/news/business/21702493-natural-gass-reputation-cleaner-fuel-coal-and-oil-risks-being-sullied-methane

Gabbert, Bill. *Wildfire Today,* "Defining fire whirls and fire tornados." August 14, 2016, wildfiretoday.com/2016/08/14/defining-fire-whirls-and-fire-tornados/

Klein, Joanna. *The New York Times,* "Watermelon Snow: Not Edible but Important for Climate Change." June 22, 2016, www.nytimes.com/2016/06/23/science/watermelon-snow-global-warming.html?_r=0

Meyer, Robinson. *The Atlantic,* "You Just Survived the Hottest Month Ever, Again." September 13, 2016, www.theatlantic.com/notes/2016/09/the-hottest-august-ever/499847/

Nace, Trevor, Contributor. *Forbes,* "Study Finds East Coast of America is Sinking into the Atlantic Ocean." September 12, 2017, https://www.forbes.com/sites/trevornace/2017/09/12/study-finds-the-east-coast-of-america-is-sinking-into-the-atlantic-ocean

National Oceanography Centre. *Science Daily,* "Microplastics discovered in the deep, open ocean." August 26, 2016, www.sciencedaily.com/releases/2016/08/160826084034.htm

Neuhauser, Alan. *U.S.News & World Report*, "Nuclear Plants Leak Radiation, and Regulator Faces Scrutiny." March 15, 2016, www.usnews.com/news/articles/2016-03-15/nuclear-plants-leak-radiation-and-regulator-faces-scrutiny

Schuttenhelm, Rolf. *bits of science*, "Climate Change & Anthropocene Extinction 24: Insects Germany declined by 76% in just 27 years (!)." Posted October 19, 2017, http://www.bitsofscience.org/anthropocene-extinction-insects-germany-decline-7553/

SECORE International, "Coral reefs are dying." http://www.secore.org/site/home/detail/coral-reefs-are-dying.1.html

Weaver, Scott. *EDF: Environmental Defense Fund*, "We just had five 1,000-year floods in less than a year. What's going on?" September 1, 2016, https://www.edf.org/blog/2016/09/01/we-just-had-five-1000-year-floods-less-year-whats-going?

Wikipedia, "List of pipeline accidents in the United States in the 21st century." en.wikipedia.org/wiki/List_of_pipeline_accidents_in_the_United_States_in_the_21st_century

About the Author

Karen Neuberg's poems and collages have appeared in numerous journals, including *805, 99 Pine Street, Forage, Hermeneutic Chaos Journal, JuxtaProse Literary Magazine, TXTOBJX,* and *Unbroken Journal;* and in anthologies including First *Water: The Best of Pirene's Fountain, A Slant of Light: Contemporary Women Writers of the Hudson Valley,* and *Words Fly Away: Poems for Fukushima.* She is a multiple Pushcart and a Best-of the Net nominee, holds an MFA from The New School, and is associate editor of the online poetry journal *First Literary Review East.* She is the author of two previous chapbooks: *Detailed Still* (Poets Wear Prada) and *Myself Taking Stage* (Finishing Line Press), and lives in Brooklyn, New York.

Glass Lyre Press

exceptional works to replenish the spirit

Glass Lyre Press is an independent literary publisher interested in technically accomplished, stylistically distinct, and original work. Glass Lyre seeks diverse writers that possess a dynamic aesthetic and an ability to emotionally and intellectually engage a wide audience of readers.

Glass Lyre's vision is to connect the world through language and art. We hope to expand the scope of poetry and short fiction for the general reader through exceptionally well-written books, which evoke emotion, provide insight, and resonate with the human spirit.

Poetry Collections
Poetry Chapbooks
Select Short & Flash Fiction
Anthologies

www.GlassLyrePress.com

www.ingramcontent.com/pod-product-compliance
Lightning Source LLC
Chambersburg PA
CBHW021200080526
44588CB00008B/435